COMMUNITY
STUDY GUIDE

POLICING
A CONTEMPORARY
PERSPECTIVE

Victor E. Kappeler

Eastern Kentucky University

California State University San Bernardino

Prepared by Karen S. Miller

 LexisNexis®

 anderson publishing
A member of the LexisNexis Group

Community Policing: A Contemporary Perspective, Fourth Edition
STUDY GUIDE

Cover design by Tin Box Studio, Inc./Cincinnati, Ohio

EDITOR Janice Eccleston
ACQUISITIONS EDITOR Michael C. Braswell

Introduction

This student Study Guide is designed to assist you in learning and reviewing the information and concepts presented in *Community Policing: A Contemporary Perspective*, Fourth Edition by Victor E. Kappeler and Larry K. Gaines. It is constructed to assist you as you prepare for exams and to help you retain the information in the text. This student Study Guide will aid you in reviewing the information from the text and allow you to test your understanding of the material. It is an instrument that will allow you to practice applying the concepts presented in each chapter. To effectively complete the exercises presented in this guide, you must first read each chapter in the text carefully.

This guide contains a section for each chapter in the text, and each section provides the following: learning objectives, a chapter outline, a review of key terms, matching and review questions, and practical exercises.

Learning Objectives

This section highlights the important topics covered in each chapter and represents the information you should have retained from reading each chapter.

Outline

The chapter outline provides you with the structure of each chapter.

Review of Key Terms

This section directs you toward the major concepts and definitions in each chapter. It contains practice questions designed to test you on the key terms from each chapter. (Answers for this section are provided in the Answer Key at the back of this Study Guide).

Review Questions

These questions provide an instrument to test your knowledge of the material. This section contains listing and essay questions. (Answers for this section are provided in the Answer Key at the back of this Study Guide. The answers that are provided for the essay questions present the *basic elements* that should be included in each essay; in some cases, however, more thorough description can be made to illustrate what you have learned from the text).

Practical Exercises

These exercises are designed to offer you a tool for using the concepts contained in each chapter. Some are problem-solving exercises and you should be creative in working these exercises. Others are research-oriented and you should utilize library and Internet resources to assist you.

Answer Key

Correct answers to the "review of key terms" and "review questions" are provided at the end of this Guide.

Study Tips

This guide can be a useful tool for students who seek to excel in the classroom. It can aid you in studying and retaining information. However, it is not designed to be a magic bullet to help you pass an exam when you have not read the chapter or attended lecture. The following are a few techniques that may help you achieve your academic goals.

1. Read each chapter carefully. Reading the chapter is your first exposure to the material.

2. Take notes while reading, either in a separate notebook, in the margins, or with a highlighter. Using a notebook is most helpful, as you can leave space between your notes for information about that topic that may be added in the classroom. Write down any questions you have while reading.

3. Attend class and take notes. This will be your second exposure to the material. Your instructor will likely offer examples to assist your understanding of key concepts. This can be very useful and you should attempt to add these examples to your notebook to trigger your memory when studying.

4. Ask questions. This can greatly impact your performance in a class. It can lead to greater understanding of the terms and concepts.

5. Complete the exercises in this study guide. This will be your third exposure to the material. It will greatly enhance your ability to retain the information and will assist in your study efforts.

6. Study for the exams. This will be your fourth exposure to the material. Utilize your notes from reading and lecture as well as your completed exercises from this guide to study.

Contents

Chapter 1
The Idea of Community Policing

Learning Objectives

After reading the chapter, you should be able to:

1. Discuss the ways in which the community impacts the police mandate when a department has implemented community policing.

2. Describe why community policing encourages decentralized police service and changes in patrol.

3. Discuss the sources of confusion surrounding the implementation of community policing.

4. List and describe the four major facets of community policing.

5. Understand why community policing is an overarching philosophy, not a technique.

6. Discuss how community policing entails the use of discretion and working with other agencies to find other means of dealing with problematic situations.

7. List and discuss what community policing does NOT constitute.

8. Discuss how community policing is sometimes used as a cover for aggressive police tactics.

9. Describe how community policing affects officer activity.

Chapter Outline

I. **The Community Policing Revolution**
   A. Philosophy
   B. Organizational Strategy
   C. Violent Crime Control and Law Enforcement Act of 1994
   D. Confusion Surrounding Community Policing

II. **The Philosophical and Structural Aspects of Community Policing**
   A. The Philosophical Facet
      1. Broad Police Function and Community Focus
      2. Citizen Input

        3.   Concern for Citizens
        4.   Developing Trust
        5.   Sharing Power
        6.   Creativity
        7.   Neighborhood Variation
        8.   The Organizational and Personnel Facet

B.   The Strategic Facet
        1.   Geographic Focus and Ownership
        2.   Direct, Daily, Face-to-Face Contact
        3.   Prevention Focus

C.   The Programmatic Facet
        1.   Reoriented Police Operations
        2.   Problem-Solving and Situational Crime Prevention
        3.   Community Engagement

III.   What Community Policing Does Not Constitute

    A.   Community Policing Is Not a Technique
    B.   Community Policing Is Not Public Relations
    C.   Community Policing Is Not Soft on Crime
    D.   Community Policing Is Not Flamboyant
    E.   Community Policing Is Not Paternalistic
    F.   Community Policing Is Not an Independent Entity
    G.   Community Policing Is Not Cosmetic
    H.   Community Policing Is Not Social Work
    I.   Community Policing Is Not Elitist
    J.   Community Policing Is Not Designed to Favor Powerful Communities
    K.   Community Policing Is Not a Panacea
    L.   Community Policing Is Not "Safe"
    M.   Community Policing Is Not a Series or Bundle of Programs
    N.   Community Policing Is Not Merely Problem-Oriented Policing

IV.   Reconciling Law Enforcement with Community Policing

V.   Summary

Review of Key Terms

aggressive tactics
community engagement
community policing
decentralize
fear of crime
law enforcement function
order maintenance
organizational and personnel facet
philosophical facet
philosophy

proactive
professional model
program facet
situational crime prevention
strategic facet
problem-oriented policing
Broken Windows theory
zero tolerance

1. _____ rests on the belief that only by working together will people and the police be able to improve quality of life.

2. The _____ of implementing community policing must be operationalized through: reoriented police operations, problem-solving and situational crime prevention, and community engagement.

3. The use of _____ causes confusion about a police department's true commitment to community policing.

4. Community policing dictates that the police be _____ rather than reactive to problems and situations.

5. The _____ of policing dictated that officers remain detached from the citizen-clients they served.

6. Community policing de-emphasizes the law enforcement function and emphasizes _____ and the provision of services to the public.

7. _____ infers that the police must work with citizens and citizen groups.

8. _____ postulates that if unchecked, a neighborhood in decline will continue to decline and the number of disorder and crime problems will increase.

9. Community policing embodies a new organizational strategy that allows police departments to _____ police service and reorient patrol.

10. The _____ of implementing community policing involves: geographic focus and ownership, direct daily face-to-face contact, and a prevention focus.

11. _____ without community policing retains the traditional authoritarian top-down approach to social problems and does not involve the power sharing necessary to make real changes in the community.

12. Community policing is a dramatic change in _____ that determines the way law enforcement agencies interact with the public.

13. The _____ of implementing community policing consists of a number of community-based elements that differentiate it from the traditional professional model.

14. In New York City, the police began enforcing previously ignore minor infractions as part of their _____ policing.

15. Community policing dictates that departments move from _____ as the primary function.

16. The _____ of community policing involves philosophical changes in the mission as well as a commitment to structural changes.

17. _____ has a far greater debilitating effect on a community than does crime rates.

18. _____ comprises opportunity-reducing measures that are directed at highly specific forms of crime, involve the management, design or manipulation of environment and increase the effort and risks of crime a perceived by offenders.

Review Questions

1. Describe how the philosophy of community policing affects the police mission.

    _____

    _____

    _____

    _____

    _____

    _____

    _____

    _____

2. List the six sources of confusion surrounding community policing.

    (1) _____

    (2) _____

    (3) _____

    (4) _____

    (5) _____

    (6) _____

3. List the seven community-based elements in the philosophical facet of community policing.

    (1) _____

    (2) _____

    (3) _____

    (4) _____

    (5) _____

    (6) _____

    (7) _____

4. List the three strategic dimensions of community policing.

    (1) _____

    (2) _____

    (3) _____

5. List the three strategies through which community policing is operationalized.

    (1) _____

    (2) _____

    (3) _____

6. List 14 things that community policing is NOT.

    (1) _____

    (2) _____

    (3) _____

    (4) _____

    (5) _____

    (6) _____

    (7) _____

    (8) _____

    (9) _____

    (10) _____

    (11) _____

    (12) _____

    (13) _____

    (14) _____

7. Describe the "weed and seed" strategy.

_____

_____

_____

_____

Practical Exercises

1. Contact your local municipal police department and sheriff's department. Ask a representative if they have implemented community policing. Ask what community policing means to them and for examples of community policing strategies. Analyze the information provided and determine if they have truly adopted the philosophy of community policing. Decide what steps they need to take to better implement the principles of community policing.

2. Read a local newspaper and locate police related stories. From these articles determine if the local police community is practicing the principles of community policing. Describe the likely police response to these situations in a department that had internalized the philosophy of community policing.

3. Use the principles and philosophy of community policing in deciding what you would do in the following situation:

    You are an officer in a medium-sized city that has adopted the community policing model. You have been assigned foot patrol in an impoverished neighborhood. You have heard citizens voice concerns about problems with noise and loitering by youth in the late afternoon hours. What steps would you take to alleviate citizen concerns and how would you deal with the youths?

Chapter 2
A History of Community Policing

Learning Objectives

After reading the chapter, you should be able to:

1. List and discuss the five interrelated pressures that influenced the historical shift from informal to formal policing in America.

2. Describe the development of policing in England

3. Describe the development of policing in America.

4. Describe the spoils system and the problems with policing during this era.

5. List and describe the three rationalizations of vigilantism.

6. Discuss the impact of the Volstead Act on police corruption.

7. List August Vollmer's 10 principles of police reform.

8. Discuss the problematic relationship police have historically had with minorities.

9. Describe the role of the 1960s in the birth of community policing.

10. List the factors that set the stage for community policing.

Chapter Outline

I. **The Lessons of History**
   A. Shift from Informal to Formal Policing

II. **Policing's British Roots**
   A. Three Periods of Policing in England
   B. Alfred the Great
   C. Edward I
   D. Industrial Revolution
   E. Sir Robert Peel
      1. Metropolitan Police Act of 1829

III. Colonial Law Enforcement in Cities and Towns
   A. Watch Systems
   B. Industrial Revolution

IV. The Rise of Municipal Police
   A. Population Growth
   B. Rioting in Major Cities
   C. Spoils System
      1. Graft and Corruption

V. Frontier Justice
   A. Westward Expansion

VI. Vigilantism
   A. Rationalizations of Vigilantism
      1. Self-Preservation
      2. Right of Revolution
      3. Economic Rationale
   B. Ku Klux Klan

VII. Twentieth-Century Policing
   A. Civil Service Reform
   B. Departmental Structural Problems
   C. High Turnover Rates
   D. Boston Police Strike
   E. Corruption

VIII. Police Reform in the 1930s
   A. August Vollmer
      1. Principles of Police Reform
   B. J. Edgar Hoover and the FBI
   C. Technology and Management Theory

IX. The Police and Minorities
   A. Immigrants
   B. African-Americans
   C. Hispanics
   D. Asian-Americans

X. Initial Attempts to Reach the Community
   A. Police Community Relations (PCR) Efforts
      1. The National Institute on Community and Police Relations
      2. Structural Weaknesses

XI. The Challenge of the Late 1960s
   A. Optimism of the Early 1960s
   B. Chaos of the Late 1960s
      1. Civil Rights Movement
      2. Vietnam War

Review of Key Terms

August Vollmer
blue laws
Civil Rights Act of 1871
Civil Service
Crime Prevention Units (CPU)
Industrial Revolution
isolation
justice of the peace
Kerner Commission
Law Enforcement Assistance Act (LEAA)
Metropolitan Police Act of 1829
New Left
Police Community Relations (PCR)
self-preservation
Sir Robert Peel
Spoils Era
team policing
vigilantism
Volstead Act of 1919

1. The _____ refers to a time when police departments were politically owned and did the bidding of politicians.

2. _____ is known as the father of modern policing.

3. _____ is the idea that citizens must be willing to kill or be killed, when the official system fails to provide adequate protection.

4. The _____ influenced the establishment of policing in England and America because it accelerated the pace of social change as people flocked to cities.

5. As head of the National Commission on Law Observance and Enforcement in 1929, _____ supervised the preparation of ten principles of police reform.

6. The _____ passed in large part because of involvement of law enforcement in the activities of the Ku Klux Klan.

7. The first official split of the judicial and law enforcement functions in England occurred when Edward II established the office of _____.

8. The first Metropolitan Police District in England was established by the _____.

9. The _____ was a loose coalition of groups clamoring for a variety of social changes.

10. _____ officers traditionally made presentations at schools and served as the liaison to other public and private agencies.

11. Prohibition of alcohol was established by the _____.

12. _____ was an effort in the early 1970s to maintain a permanent team of officers in a particular geographic area.

13. The 1950s saw the introduction of _____, a proactive approach aimed at the community.

14. Changes in hiring and promotion practices occurred as a result of _____ reform.

15. One factor that set the stage for community policing was the _____ of police in patrol cars.

16. When citizens pursue suspected felons, they are assisting the police, but when they seek to inflict punishment, they have crossed the line into _____.

17. Police response to protestors at the 1968 Democratic convention was later called a police riot by the _____.

18. New technology for police departments was funded by the _____.

19. A peculiarly American phenomenon where religious groups successfully lobbied to make custom part of the criminal law is referred to as _____.

Review Questions

1. List the five interrelated pressures that impacted the historical shift from informal to formal policing.

    (1) _____

    (2) _____

    (3) _____

    (4) _____

    (5) _____

2. List the three distinct, successive periods of the history of law enforcement in England.

    (1) _____

    (2) _____

    (3) _____

3. Describe the Spoils Era in American history.

_____

_____

_____

_____

_____

_____

_____

4. List and define the three rationalizations for vigilantism.

    (1) _____

    (2) _____

    (3) _____

5. List the 10 principles of reform as established by August Vollmer and the National Commission on Law Observance and Enforcement.

    (1) _____

    (2) _____

    (3) _____

    (4) _____

    (5) _____

    (6) _____

    (7) _____

    (8) _____

    (9) _____

    (10) _____

6. List the seven areas Kelling and Moore argue were revolutionized by the work of Vollmer and Wilson.

    (1) _____

    (2) _____

    (3) _____

    (4) _____

    (5) _____

    (6) _____

    (7) _____

7. List the seven objectives of a good Police Community Relations program as outlined in 1955 by the National Institute on Community and Police Relations.

    (1) _____

    (2) _____

    (3) _____

    (4) _____

    (5) _____

    (6) _____

    (7) _____

8. List the primary issues that had a negative impact on police/community relations in the 1960s.

    _____

    _____

    _____

    _____

    _____

    _____

    _____

    _____

9. What are the two common themes shared by the factors that set the stage for the birth of community policing?

    (1) _____

    (2) _____

Practical Exercises

1. The text mentions a series of riots that occurred in the 1800s in many major cities. Choose two of these riots and research them to determine the events that lead to both and the official response to them. What do you think would have happened if state response had been different? Would they have been as deadly or would property damage have been as extensive? How do you believe these police departments would respond to these situations today?

2. Watch movies from various decades in the 1900s that have police related plots. How were the police portrayed in different eras? Using the information from your text determine whether or not the portrayal was accurate and deserved.

3. You have been assigned to supervise the new community policing initiative in your 300-officer department. You are having difficulty with several of your white CPOs who are facing animosity from their predominately African-American beats. They are losing hope of successfully becoming a part of these communities and are experiencing difficulty gaining the trust of the citizens.

4. Your job is to use the information provided in this chapter and write a narrative of the history between the police and the African-American community. Make these officers understand how what began with slave patrols in the south, continued through the centuries causing death and injury to many African-Americans at the hands of law enforcement officials. Explain the history and make clear its role in the modern relationship between African-Americans and the police.

Chapter 3
The Changing Meaning of Community

Learning Objectives

After reading the chapter, you should be able to:

1. Understand the importance of defining community.

2. Understand how communities have changed over the course of time.

3. Describe differing definitions of community and list their common elements.

4. Understand the difference between community and neighborhood.

5. Describe the historical development of suburbs.

6. List the factors that have contributed to a growing underclass in American society.

7. Describe the role of technology in the evolution of community.

8. List and describe the three-tiered "hierarchy of community" based on class.

9. Discuss the police role in building a sense of community.

Chapter Outline

I.   The Importance of Definitions

II.   A History of the Meaning of Community
   A.   The Definition of Community
        1.   German Sociologist Tönnies 1887
        2.   1930s
        3.   1950s
   B.   Neighborhood
   C.   Elements of Communities

III. Assaults on Community
   A.   American Community
   B.   American Society
   C.   Suburbs
   D.   Economic Shifts

IV. **The Technological and Corporate Divide**
     A.   Affordable Technology
     B.   Multinational Corporations
     C.   Mass Media
     D.   Kurt Vonnegut
     E.   Hierarchy of Community

V.   **How Community Policing Can Build a Sense of Community**
     A.   Improving the Quality of Life
     B.   Engaging the Community

VI. **Summary**

Review of Key Terms

adversarial
blockbusting
Chicago School
community relationships
hierarchy
inclusion
initiatives
Kurt Vonnegut
legal constructs
natural community
neighborhood
social interactions
threat of crime
underclass

   1. In contrast to the _____ relationship in the traditional system, the
      community policing philosophy encourages the department to humanize all inter-
      actions with citizens.

   2. _____ was a real estate practice that prompted white homeown-
      ers into selling because of the fear that African-American families moving in
      would cause property values to plunge.

   3. A welcome by-product of community policing is improved race relations,
      exclusion produces conflict while _____ builds communities.

   4. The _____ can be a catalyst to make people see that they do
      share a community of interest based on mutual geography.

   5. Technological and corporate changes have accentuated the _____
      of community based on class.

6. Economic shifts have contributed to a growing _____ in American society, more than one-fourth of American families now live in poverty.

7. The _____ technique of defining community relied on identifying central locators, such as businesses, churches, and schools, and then drawing the boundary lines.

8. _____ must come from the community and not just from police or elites attempting to impose their vision of community.

9. Police have the ability to change _____ and invoke processes that directly affect the quality of community life.

10. German sociologist Tönnies made a clear distinction between _____ that were defined by intimacy and those that were based on achievement.

11. In the 1930s social scientists began focusing their definitions on _____ of community.

12. Language and shared symbols help identify the _____.

13. A _____ is a small physical area embedded within a larger area in which people inhabit dwellings.

14. _____ argues that the craving for community runs so deep that it is a factor in drug use.

Review Questions

1. Define community in the "concrete" sense.

_____

_____

_____

_____

_____

_____

_____

_____

_____

_____

_____

2. List the eight common elements of the various definitions of community.

   (1) _____

   (2) _____

   (3) _____

   (4) _____

   (5) _____

   (6) _____

   (7) _____

   (8) _____

3. List the six features that may be indicative of a community.

   _____

   _____

   _____

   _____

   _____

   _____

   _____

4. Describe the role of technology in the evolving sense of community.

   _____

   _____

   _____

   _____

   _____

   _____

   _____

5. List and describe the three-tiered hierarchy of community, based on class.

   _____

   _____

   _____

   _____

   _____

   _____

6. What is the role of the police in developing a sense of community?

_____

_____

_____

_____

_____

_____

_____

_____

_____

_____

7. Where do community policing efforts start?

_____

_____

_____

_____

_____

_____

_____

Practical Exercises

1. Crime, fear of crime, and disorder contribute to the lack of a sense of community. Identify an area in your hometown that meets these criteria. Develop a plan for the local police department to encourage a sense of community in that area. Determine the following: Who is included in that community? Who should you first approach in the community? What concerns will likely be voiced by residents? What is your goal?

2. Informally interview friends and family who live in different areas of your city or town. Ask them to describe what community means to them. Find common characteristics and compare them to those presented in the text. Determine if their behavior indicates a sense of community and if they would be responsive to community policing efforts.

3. Map your city or town and determine if you see a pattern of hierarchy based on class. How do you think this developed? Do you see patterns of racial or ethnic segregation? What historical factors influenced this pattern?

4. Use the principles and philosophy of community policing in deciding what should be done in the following situation:

    You are a Community Policing Officer in a medium-sized city. A neighborhood has banded together to offer support to one of its residents who was arrested for animal cruelty. He had been operating a dog breeding business and had more than 50 dogs who were underfed and dirty, but not otherwise mistreated. His neighbors are arguing that he has a right to run his business on his property and supplement his income in this way. A larger community of animal rights activists from across the city is protesting and arguing that the animals are being mistreated as a result of their living conditions. Both "communities" are pressing the police department to deal with this situation.

    Identify your goals and determine a plan for how best to deal with this situation.

Chapter 4
The Police and Public

Learning Objectives

After reading the chapter, you should be able to:

1. Understand micro explanations of citizens' views of the police.
2. Understand the benefits to both the police and community when good relations exist.
3. Describe how age tends to affect citizens' attitudes toward police.
4. Describe how gender tends to affect citizens' attitudes toward police.
5. Describe how race tends to affect citizens' attitudes toward police.
6. Describe how socioeconomic status tends to affect citizen attitudes toward police.
7. Describe how personal experience tends to affect citizens' attitudes toward police.
8. Discuss the barriers to good police-community relations.

Chapter Outline

I. **Citizen Attitudes Toward the Police**
   A. Woldview
   B. Culture
   C. Benefits of Good Relations Between Police and Community

II. **How Age Affects Citizens' Perceptions of the Police**

III. **How Race Affects Citizens' Perceptions of the Police**

IV. **How Gender Affects Citizens' Perceptions of the Police**

V. **How Socioeconomic Status Affects Citizens' Perceptions of the Police**

VI. **How Personal Experience Affects Citizen's Perceptions of the Police**

VII. Barriers to a Police-Community Partnership
    A.   Excessive Force
    B.   Police Corruption
    C.   Rudeness
    D.   Authoritarianism
    E.   Politics

VIII. Summary

Review of Key Terms

Symbolic assailants
Non-confrontive communication skills
Socioeconomic status
Excessive force
Mollen Commission
Police corruption
Rampart scandal
authoritarianism

1. Officers should be trained on _____ to reduce friction with young people.

2. An individual's social and economic class is referred to as their _____.

3. The notion that police officers tend to become corrupt over time through progressive stages was recognized by _____.

4. _____ is an attitude or approach used when exercising authority and is typically seen as negative or coercive.

5. The _____ in Los Angeles caused many in the community to wonder whether police were planting evidence and lying in court.

6. One way police officers tend to stereotype is to view citizens as _____.

7. Proper training of police officers can reduce _____, which can in turn improve relations with the community.

8. The illegal drug industry embodies such vast amounts of money that numerous opportunities exist for officers to engage in _____.

Review Questions

1. Describe why it is important for the public to view the police positively.

    _____

    _____

    _____

    _____

    _____

    _____

    _____

2. List the seven benefits to the police and community when good relations exist.

    (1) _____

    (2) _____

    (3) _____

    (4) _____

    (5) _____

    (6) _____

    (7) _____

3. Describe how and why age affects citizen's perceptions of the police.

    _____

    _____

    _____

    _____

    _____

    _____

    _____

4. Describe how and why race affects citizens' perceptions of police.

    _____

    _____

    _____

    _____

    _____

    _____

5. Is there a difference in how males and females view police? What about socioe-
    conomic status?

    _____

    _____

    _____

    _____

    _____

    _____

6. List and briefly describe the five barriers to a police-community partnership

    _____

    _____

    _____

    _____

    _____

Practical Exercises

1. As an officer in a midsize city, you have been assigned to identify the popula-
    tions that view your department and its activities in a negative way. Develop a
    plan that will help you identify the populations, determine how you would sur-
    vey them about their attitudes, and then based on the information in the text,
    determine what the department can do to improve these relationships.

2. Watch three films that portray the police role in the war on drugs, and three
    episodes of any police reality show or television series. Write an essay describ-
    ing the ways the police and the drug dealers are presented. Discuss how these
    portrayals may impact citizen views of police.

3. Using the four areas that police administrators should consider to improve rela-
    tions with the public, develop a plan for the police department in your home
    community. Identify the primary demographic group that may view the police
    most negatively and determine which of the areas your local police agency
    should address to improve relations with citizens.

Chapter 5
Managing Community Policing

Learning Objectives

After reading the chapter, you should be able to:

1. Understand the historical role of the military model in policing.

2. List the six principles of classical organizational theory.

3. Understand and define organic organization.

4. Describe the best way to organize a department for community policing.

5. Describe how organizational culture can hinder the implementation of community policing.

6. List and describe the four factors of comprehensive change.

7. Identify and describe the eight steps of implementing community policing.

Chapter Outline

I. **Organizing the Police**
   A. Serving the Public

II. **Principles of Organization and Police Administration**
   A. Military Model

III. **Classical Organization Principles**
   A. Max Weber
      1. Six Principles of Classical Organizational Theory
   B. Organic Organizations
   C. Changing Leadership
   D. Officer Commitment

IV. **Organizing for Community Policing**

V.   Strategic Planning
- A.   Establishing Goals
- B.   Building Relationships
- C.   Developing Lines of Communication
    1.   Neighborhood Counsels
    2.   Chief's Advisory Committee
    3.   Special Committees
- D.   Improving Communication in the Department
    1.   Command or Administrative Staff Meetings
    2.   Quality Circles
    3.   Unit Meetings

VI.   COMPSTAT
- A.   Reports
- 1.   The COMPSTAT Report
- 2.   The Commander profile Report
- 3.   The Crime Mapping Report

VII.   Personnel Development
- A.   Training

VIII.   Tactical Planning and Operations
- A.   Supervision
    1.   Four Types of Supervisors
- B.   Geographical Focus
- C.   Reoriented Police Operations and Problem Solving

IX.   Implementing Community-Oriented Policing
- A.   Step 1: Performance Gap
- B.   Step 2: Recognizing a Need for Change
- C.   Step 3: Creating a Proper Climate for Change
- D.   Step 4: Diagnosing the Problem
- E.   Step 5: Identifying Alternative Strategies
- F.   Step 6: Selecting the Strategy
- G.   Step 7: Determining and Operationalizing Implementation Strategy
- H.   Step 8: Evaluating and Modifying the Strategy

XI.   Summary

Review of Key Terms

authority
active supervisors
bean counting
classical organizational theory
commander profile report
community partnership
comprehensive model

COMPSTAT
division of labor
evaluating
leadership
neighborhood counsels
organic organizations
problem solving
quality circles
role
structure
territorial imperative

1. Police _____ must be changed if community policing is to be successful, administrators must be committed to it.

2. Police typically envision their _____ as one of law enforcement.

3. Police organization is about how to _____ the department so that departmental goals and objectives are achieved.

4. The _____ attempts to introduce community policing concepts and techniques throughout the department.

5. _____ are often comprised of religious leaders, business people, community activists, and ordinary citizens who have community concerns.

6. _____ is a managerial process that uses crime analysis information, and periodic meetings to discuss crime problems.

7. Specialization or _____ exists whereby individuals are assigned a limited number of job tasks and responsibilities.

8. _____ often make arrests and write citations working in the field, because they have not yet accepted the fact that they are supervisors.

9. The principles of _____ provide a high degree of structure and sometimes result in employees behaving as bureaucrats.

10. Upper and middle management are responsible for _____ and modifying community policing once it is in place.

11. When officers come to know and associate with the area and people they patrol or police, it is referred to as: _____.

12. _____ are more open and delegate higher levels of responsibility to subordinates at the operational levels.

13. The _____ is a report card on how managers are dealing with their crime problems and their units.

14. _____ are formed to deal with significant problems in a department such as use of force or changes in policies.

15. _____ within the organization is associated with one's position.

16. Two essential elements of community policing are _____ and _____.

17. Many police departments rely on _____ bean counting _____, or making large numbers of arrests without considering whether such activities improve the community.

Review Questions

1. List the six principles that have become the foundation of classical organizational theory.

    (1) _____

    (2) _____

    (3) _____

    (4) _____

    (5) _____

    (6) _____

2. List the five possible responses to calls for service.

    (1) _____

    (2) _____

    (3) _____

    (4) _____

    (5) _____

3. List and define the four types of police supervisors.

    (1) _____

    (2) _____

    (3) _____

    (4) _____

4. List the eight steps of implementing community policing.

    (1) _____

    (2) _____

    (3) _____

    (4) _____

    (5) _____

    (6) _____

    (7) _____

    (8) _____

Practical Exercises

1. Choose an organization in your community (a church, fast food restaurant, university, etc.) and identify how it has implemented the six principles of classical organizational theory.

2. Locate a local law enforcement organization that has implemented community policing. Arrange an interview with a high-ranking officer and ask about the structural and organizational changes made to facilitate the implementation. Ask about the obstacles the department faced in this process. Ask about any evaluation procedures currently utilized.

3. Using the eight steps provided in the text, design a plan for implementing community policing for a 10-officer department and for a 500-officer department. Keep in mind the different organizational structures that would likely already be in place (i.e., specialized units and more middle managers in the larger department). Identify the problem areas that would be faced by the larger department.

4. As an administrator in a mid-size department, you have been charged with educating your colleagues about COMPSTAT. Use information from the text and other sources to write an essay describing its functions, weaknesses, and benefits.

Chapter 6
Problem Solving and Community Policing

Learning Objectives

After reading the chapter, you should be able to:

1. Understand the concept of problem solving.

2. Delineate the differences between traditional reactive policing and problem solving.

3. Describe the role of geography and hot spots in problem solving.

4. Describe the SARA model.

5. Understand the methods for identifying problems.

6. Understand the role of the community in identifying and solving problems.

7. Describe the reasons police departments do not engage in problem solving.

Chapter Outline

I.   **The Nature of Problems and Problem Solving**
    A.   Spatial Segregation
    B.   Differences Between Reactive Policing and Problem Solving

II. **Geographical Policing**
    A.   Dangerous Places

III. **Defining Hot Spots or Problem Areas**
    A.   Citizen and Police Behavior

IV. **The Mechanics of Problem Solving**
    A.   Scanning
        1.   Identifying Hot Spots
    B.   Analysis
        1.   Collecting Information
    C.   Response
        1.   Engaging Citizens

D.   Assessment
1.   Evaluate Results

V.   Methods for Identifying Problems
A.   Officer Observation and Experience
1.   Patrol Officers
2.   Community Partnerships
3.   Polling Officers
B.   Citizen Complaints and Community Groups
1.   Citizen Discussion Forums
2.   Benefits of Community Meetings
C.   Crime Mapping
1.   CAD/RMS
2.   Activities for a Particular Shift or Watch
3.   Activities for a Particular Beat or Police District
4.   Activities Around a "Hot Spot" or Concentration of Crime and Disorder
5.   Concentrations of Activities in an Area Over Time
6.   Compare Police Activities with Social and Ecological Characteristics
D.   Police Reports, Calls for Service Analysis, and Crime Analysis
1.   Geographic Concentration Pattern
a.   Crime and Related Activities
2.   Similar Offense Pattern
E.   Citizen Surveys
1.   Lexington, Kentucky
2.   Tempe, Arizona

VI.   Police Problem Solving
A.   Drug Trafficking
1.   New York, New York
2.   Lexington, Kentucky
3.   San Diego, California
B.   Burglaries
1.   Nassau County, New York
2.   Fontana, California

VII.   Why Police Departments Do Not Engage in Problem Solving
A.   Officers Lack the Analytical Skills Needed
B.   Managers and Supervisors Do Not Know How
C.   Agencies Resist Change
D.   Heavy Workloads
E.   Little Community Involvement
F.   Little Support for Governmental Agencies
G.   Circumstantial Problems
H.   Linear Process
I.   Too Little is Known About the Problem

VIII. Summary

Review of Key Terms

citizen surveys
community meetings
community partnerships
crime analysis
dangerous place
geographic concentration pattern
hot spot
New York City Police Department
Newport News, Virginia
problem solving
prevention efforts
problems
reactive
response
scanning
societal problems
third party policing

1. Crime and disorder problems are the result of innumerous _____ that are outside the control of the police.

2. The _____ is where a number of crimes or activities are concentrated in a specific geographical area.

3. A _____ describes a concentration of crime and disorder.

4. Once a problem or hot spot is clearly identified, the police must then structure an effective _____.

5. As a part of building _____ patrol officers can develop positive relationships with citizens in the areas they patrol.

6. _____ are a way of measuring citizen attitudes about the police and police performance.

7. _____ serve as an excellent opportunity to gather information and develop better relations with citizens.

8. _____ must focus on specific problems as opposed to distributing efforts randomly.

9. One example of using problem-solving techniques occurred in _____ following high rates of thefts from automobiles in parking lots near the shipyards.

10. The factors which are useful in the _____ function include types of crimes, times of occurrence, locations of occurrence, suspect information, victim information, modus operandi, and physical evidence.

11. Social, health, and quality-of-life problems and issues are all the providence of police _____.

12. _____ are a cluster of incidents or calls for service and crime that are of concern to the police and the public.

13. A _____ is a location that attracts criminals and results in high levels of crime and disorder.

14. Problem-solving techniques were utilized by _____ to eliminate drug trafficking in a park by working with citizens.

15. Historically, the police have been _____, thus they depended on community members to call when a problem arose.

16. _____ refers to a process whereby individual officers, units, or department collectively examine a jurisdiction for problems.

17. When officers and departments offer solutions that involve other governmental agencies it is referred to as _____.

Review Questions

1. Describe the differences between traditional reactive policing and problem solving.

   _____

   _____

   _____

   _____

   _____

   _____

   _____

   _____

   _____

   _____

   _____

2.   Describe the SARA model of problem solving.

_____

_____

_____

_____

_____

_____

_____

_____

3.   List the methods of identifying problems.

_____

_____

_____

_____

_____

_____

_____

_____

_____

_____

_____

4.   List the six ways police are able to view activities for the purposes of crime mapping.

(1) _____

(2) _____

(3) _____

(4) _____

(5) _____

(6) _____

5.   What are the two broad types of crime patterns?

(1) _____

(2) _____

6. List the nine reasons police agencies do not engage in problem solving activities.

(1) _____

(2) _____

(3) _____

(4) _____

(5) _____

(6) _____

(7) _____

(8) _____

(9) _____

Practical Exercises

1. As a police officer in a medium-sized city who is assigned a beat that includes two subdivisions, you have noticed an increase in calls involving vandalism and minor theft. You have noticed that the items being vandalized and broken into are mostly automobiles that are parked on the street. The items being stolen are stereos and CDs. A large majority of these thefts are occurring in the late afternoon hours.

    Using the SARA model of problem solving, design a plan for eliminating or reducing these occurrences. What patterns would you look for? Who would you contact for informational purposes? Where would you look for information? Once you have learned the "who, what, when, where, and how" of the problem, develop a response and a method for assessing your success.

2. Contact a local police official and ask him/her to describe a problem-solving experience. What process did they use? How did they involve the community? Was the plan successful? How do they monitor their success?

3. Your department has identified a "hot spot" involving drug sales and use. This "hot spot" is a park in an area characterized by high poverty and crime rates. The residential area on one side of the park is made up predominately of Hispanics and on the other, African-Americans. Each group of citizens blames the other for the park becoming dilapidated and the children not having an area to play. The park is in poor condition, most of the playground equipment is broken, and the basketball courts are not useable due to broken concrete and missing goals. The area has not been landscaped and is overrun by weeds. Many of the streetlights do not function properly and homeless people sleep on the few benches that are left.

As a police officer in this large city, you have been assigned to develop a plan for solving these problems. Establish your goals and develop a plan for eliminating the drug use and sales from the park and providing the children of these communities a place to play. How would you resolve the conflict between the two communities? Would this be necessary? Why? What social service organizations would you involve in your efforts? Why? What would you do to maintain your success over time?

4. You have been assigned the task of developing a crime mapping program for your department. Using information from the text and other sources, develop a plan for this task. What information is necessary? Will new personnel be needed? What types of software are available? How will crime mapping help your department?

Chapter 7
Community Policing and Crime

Learning Objectives

After reading the chapter, you should be able to:

1. List the four methods of evaluating police performance.

2. Understand the purpose and limitations of the Uniform Crime Report (UCR).

3. Describe the results of the Canadian study on the impact of bank robberies versus stolen bikes performed by Chris Braiden.

4. List the three times when police action can influence crime.

5. Understand the differences between traditional policing and community policing in response to crime.

6. Understand and describe the significance of the Kansas City Preventive Patrol Experiment.

7. Understand and describe the significance of the RAND study.

8. Describe the ways in which community policing can impact domestic violence homicides.

9. Understand the importance of the CPO in community policing efforts.

Chapter Outline

I.   Challenges to Traditional Crime Control
    A.   Four Means of Evaluating Police Performance
        1.   Reported Crime Rates
        2.   Overall Arrests
        3.   Clearance Rates
        4.   Response Times

II.   Police Measures of Crime – What Do We Know?
    A.   Uniform Crime Report (UCR)
        1.   Index Crimes
    B.   Context of Crime

III. The Traditional Police Effort
    A. Police Impact on Crime
        1. Prevention
            a. Kansas City Preventive Patrol Study
        2. Crimes in Progress
            a. Citizen Delay in Reporting
        3. Resolving Crimes Already Committed
            a. RAND Study

IV. The Dynamics of Serious Crime
    A. Homicide
        1. Minneapolis Domestic Violence Experiment
        2. Community Policing and Domestic Violence Murders

V. Community Policing's Strengths
    A. Broadening the Police Mandate
    B. Putting Crime in Social Context
    C. Role of CPOs

Review of Key Terms

crime-fighters
context
deterrence
Index
juveniles
Kansas City Preventive Patrol study
mandate
Minneapolis Experiment
mission
motor patrol
opportunity-reduction
outreach specialists
professional policing model
RAND
rapid response
status offenses
Uniform Crime Reports

1. The rationale for having _____ is that the visible presence in the community should act as a deterrent to crime.

2. _____ does not contribute to increased apprehensions in the majority of crimes.

3. The lack of citizen response to cries for help from a woman being beaten and stabbed in New York City was viewed by many as the result of policing over-selling themselves as _____.

4. _____ are statistics compiled by the FBI that focus on the eight _____ crimes.

5. Community policing goes beyond reducing calls for service and handling minor disorders by broadening the police _____ and restructuring the department to carry out this expanded _____.

6. Supporters of traditional and modern forms of crime prevention argue, based on a _____ philosophy that police action can influence crime.

7. CPOs are considered the be the _____ of the department.

8. _____ are that are criminal for juveniles but would not be considered crimes if committed by an adult.

9. The _____ raised concerns about random motor patrol's impact on crime prevention and citizen satisfaction.

10. The _____ has been ineffective in reducing crime, reducing citizens' fears, and satisfying victims that justice is being done.

11. Involving the police in efforts aimed at _____ holds the promise of breaking down the barriers between the police and the adults in the community.

12. Nearly all of the evaluation research on collective anti-crime strategies focuses on _____ activities.

13. The _____ study cast serious doubt on criminal investigators' ability to solve crimes.

14. While the results were not replicated in other studies, the _____ showed that when police arrested domestic violence suspects repeat violence was reduced in the following six months.

15. In order for CPOs to be effective in their efforts, they must be educated in the _____, not just the control, of crime.

Review Questions

1. List the four accepted practices that are used to evaluate police performance.

   (1) _____

   (2) _____

   (3) _____

   (4) _____

2.   List the eight Index crimes focused on in the Uniform Crime Reports.

    (1) _____

    (2) _____

    (3) _____

    (4) _____

    (5) _____

    (6) _____

    (7) _____

    (8) _____

3.   List the three ways in which some researchers argue that policing can influence crime.

    (1) _____

    (2) _____

    (3) _____

4.   Describe the findings of the Kansas City Preventive Patrol Study.

_____

_____

_____

_____

_____

_____

_____

_____

_____

_____

_____

_____

_____

_____

_____

_____

_____

_____

_____

5. List the three primary reasons for citizen delays in calling the police.

    (1) _____

    (2) _____

    (3) _____

6. List the three categories of cases facing investigators.

    (1) _____

    (2) _____

    (3) _____

7. What is a primary function of long-range, proactive community policing efforts?

    _____

    _____

    _____

    _____

    _____

    _____

    _____

Practical Exercises

1. Locate various agencies in your community that provide services to victims of domestic violence. Develop a plan for the police department to best handle these types of calls for assistance using the services you feel are relevant. Keep in mind the cycle of violence and the impact witnessing violence in the home has on children. Include in your plan some method of long term prevention by offering service to children.

2. Distinguish between the likely responses to the following scenario of a department using traditional crime control measures and one using community policing tactics:

    A low-income neighborhood that is characterized by relatively low crime rates, strong community bonds, and highly religious residents has been experiencing a growing amount of gang related activity. The community has been working together for one year to eliminate graffiti and to keep the area clean. The gang members are mostly from a bordering community and have been marking this new "turf" with colorful graffiti. Residents are worried that this activity will soon lead to an increase in drug activity and most importantly to their children joining gangs.

3. The small community in which you reside and work as a CPO has recently experienced a series of thefts of street and stop signs. The thefts are occurring late at night and citizens are concerned that this presents the potential for accidents. After some investigation, you realize that the responsible parties are high school students though you have no proof of the involvement of anyone in particular. The citizens of your community aren't interested in seeing these children arrested, they only want them to stop. How can your department best deal with this situation? Determine if a law enforcement approach or an educational approach would be best suited to deal with this situation. Develop a plan for ending the thefts and appeasing the citizens. What do you think the root cause of these thefts would be and how would you deal with it?

4. As the Chief of a small police department, you have learned that the citizens in your community are upset because they perceive your department as ignoring petty crime. You must develop a plan designed to alleviate this concern. How will your increase the sensitivity among your officers toward victims of petty crime? What steps can your department take to make citizens feel better about your response to petty crimes?

Chapter 8
Community Policing and Fear of Crime

Learning Objectives

After reading the chapter, you should be able to:

1. Understand the economic and social damage done to society as a result of fear of crime.

2. Discuss the relevance of the Figgie Report and the Flint Foot Patrol Experiment.

3. Understand the roles of indirect victimization, community concern, and incivilities in citizen fear of crime.

4. Describe the demographics of those most fearful and their actual rates of victimization.

5. Discuss the relationship between victimization and fear of crime.

6. Understand the roles of the media and law enforcement in the public's heightened fear of crime.

7. Describe the response of community policing to fear of crime.

8. Discuss the relationship between socioeconomic status and fear of crime.

9. Cite the types of crimes citizens are most fearful of.

10. Describe the four theoretical models of fear of crime.

Chapter Outline

I. **Traditional Policing and Fear of Crime**
    A. Societal Damage
    B. Contemporary History

II. **Discovering the Fear of Crime**
    A. Figgie Report 1980
        1. Demographics of Those Most Fearful
        2. Formless Fear

     B.   Flint Foot Patrol Experiment
         1.   Law Enforcement Related Problems
         2.   Controversies Within Flint Police Department
         3.   Objectives

III. What Is Fear of Crime?
     A.   Irrationality
         1.   Gender and Age
         2.   Global and Specific Fears
         3.   Indirect Knowledge of Crime
     B.   Six Areas of Indirect Costs

IV. Theoretical Models Explaining Fear of Crime
     A.   The Victimization Model
     B.   The Disorder Model
     C.   The Community Concern Model
     D.   The Subcultural-Diversity Model

V. Extent of Fear of Crime
     A.   Problems Associated with Measuring
     B.   Sourcebook of Criminal Justice Statistics

VI. Victimization and Fear of Crime
     A.   Direct Victimization

VII. Gender and Fear of Crime
     A.   Victimization of Women
     B.   Role of Children

VIII. Age and Fear of Crime
     A.   Rate of Victimization
     B.   Reasons for Fear

IX. Race and Fear of Crime
     A.   Young, African-American Males
     B.   Elderly African-Americans

X. The Media and Fear of Crime
     A.   Sensational Reporting
     B.   Three Factors that Impact Fear of Crime
     C.   The Police Roles
     D.   Television Shows

XI. Personal Wealth and Fear of Crime
     A.   Minimum Loss and Inconvenience

Review of Key Terms

age
Citizen Oriented Police Enforcement (COPE)
Community Organizing Response Team (CORT)
community policing
concrete fear
fear of crime
Figgie Report
Flint Foot Patrol Experiment
formless fear
gender
law enforcement community
media
moral panics
Newark Fear Reduction Campaign
primary victimization
property crime
routine preventive patrol
secondary victimization
under-enforcement
victimization
violent crime
wealth

1. The media, as a result of slanted coverage of the news tend to start
   _____.

2. The ordering of fear of crime by age or gender results in the exact opposite of
   _____ rates.

3. While it had little impact on fear of crime, the _____ reduced perceived social disorder problems.

4. _____ activities have little impact on citizens' perception of the police and their feelings of safety.

5. The _____ was one of the first national studies to examine the level of fear of crime in the United States.

6. The _____ tends to distort coverage of crime which leads to increased fear of crime.

7. _____ generates the largest number of complaints from the African-American community.

8. _____ is an emotional reaction characterized by a sense of danger and anxiety.

9. The _____ Project in Baltimore County, Maryland, was designed to reduce citizen fear of crime.

10. _____ relates to a diffuse feeling of being unsafe as a result of crime and disorder in the immediate environment.

11. Through television programs such as "Crime Solvers," and "Crime Line" the _____ contributes to the public's unrealistic fear of crime.

12. _____ occurred when a criminal act was committed against the victim.

13. By expanding the police mission and being proactive in addressing disorder, _____ directly addresses indirect fears associated with community problems.

14. The _____ was one of the first police experiments to include fear of crime as a factor and was successful at reducing citizen fear.

15. In Houston, Texas, the _____ organized the community through block meetings and other citizen contact.

16. _____ refers to the treatment a victim receives from the criminal justice system.

17. _____ as a predictor of fear is stronger in inner cities and weakest in rural areas.

18. Fear about specific crimes is referred to as _____.

19. _____ appears to be the greatest predictor of fear of crime.

20. One factor that contributes to the ability to quickly recover from victimization is _____.

21. _____ ranks well below _____ in generating fear among Americans.

Review Questions

1. What two things historically caused the police to focus on law enforcement and contributed to police corruption?

   (1) _____

   (2) _____

2. Prior to the 1960s, what was the primary interest surrounding crime victims?

   _____

   _____

   _____

   _____

   _____

   _____

   _____

   _____

   _____

   _____

   _____

3. List the five groups that exhibit the greatest concrete fear of crime according to the Figgie Report?

   (1) _____

   (2) _____

   (3) _____

   (4) _____

   (5) _____

4. List the six groups showing the highest rates of formless fear according to the Figgie Report.

    (1) _____

    (2) _____

    (3) _____

    (4) _____

    (5) _____

    (6) _____

5. List the three inconsistencies between victimization levels and fear of crime.

    (1) _____

    (2) _____

    (3) _____

6. Identify the six areas that are the indirect costs of fear of crime in our society.

    (1) _____

    (2) _____

    (3) _____

    (4) _____

    (5) _____

    (6) _____

7. Identify the three factors that predict the influence of news reporting on fear of crime.

    (1) _____

    (2) _____

    (3) _____

8. Identify and describe the four theoretical modes of fear of crime.

    (1) _____

    _____

    (2) _____

    _____

    (3) _____

    _____

    (4) _____

    _____

Practical Exercises

1. Using the philosophy and strategies inherent in community policing, solve the following problem: A subdivision in your community is inhabited by predominantly elderly people. Many of the residents have lived in their homes for more than twenty years. They are still able to care for themselves and tend to look out for one another. As the officer assigned to this area, you have noticed a large number of calls relating to strange noises and the belief that someone is breaking into their homes. You recognize that these residents are very fearful of crime. Develop a plan for easing the fears and improving the quality of life for these residents.

2. Develop a survey instrument to measure the level of fear of crime among your fellow students. It may help you to locate a published survey from your university library. Approach some professors to get permission to survey at least four classes. Locate the most recent crime statistics from both the university and the municipality. Compare the levels of fear to the actual crime statistics. Do you see a discrepancy? Do you see patterns of fear by gender or race? Are these fears realistic? Do students who reside on campus feel more secure? What do you feel the university could do to eliminate some fears of the students?

3. As a CPO in a large department, your chief has assigned you to resolve the situation presented below. You are to work with the sexual assault unit that is investigating the crimes, but your primary role is to ease the fears of the women involved.

    In a 10-month period, six women have been sexually assaulted in public restrooms located in the buildings of large office complexes located throughout the city. Several women have quit their jobs and many more call in sick because they are afraid to go to work. The owners of the complexes and business want their employees to feel safe and want to protect themselves from liability. The promise of catching the perpetrator are falling on deaf ears and local women's groups are beginning to protest the police department. Develop a plan for easing the fears of the people involved and for reducing the animosity between the women's groups and the police.

4. A recent survey of your community revealed that local citizens are very fearful of being victimized by property crime, violent crime, and terrorism. You have been asked to give a presentation to your fellow officers describing why terrorism has suddenly appeared as a fear cited by members of your community. Use any resources available to you (i.e., newspaper articles, content of news reports, television shows, etc) to help your fellow officers understand the ways the media and politicians have contributed to this new fear. Was this fear constructed by the media and politicians in the wake of September 11, 2001? Compare the levels of fear to the reality of victimization? Is this a rational fear?

Chapter 9
Community Policing and Drugs

Learning Objectives

After reading the chapter, you should be able to:

1. Understand the nature and extent of the drug problem.

2. List the six goals that should guide police decision-making when implementing drug strategies.

3. Describe high-level and retail-level law enforcement strategies and the limitations of each.

4. Understand the importance of directing prevention efforts at juveniles.

5. Understand how community policing can use problem solving to effectively deal with the drug issue.

6. Describe how community policing can be effective at information gathering for the purpose of drug enforcement.

7. Describe how community policing drug enforcement efforts are dependent upon the public and the importance of community involvement.

8. Understand the ways that community policing can direct police responses in the war on drugs.

Chapter Outline

I.   Nature and Extent of the Drug Problem
    A.   National Drug Control Policy Use Estimates
    B.   Emergency Room Mentions

II.   Police Drug Strategies
    A.   Harm Reduction
        1.   Moore and Kleiman Six Goals of Drug Elimination Strategies
    B.   High-Level Enforcement
        1.   Federal Agencies
        2.   Interdiction
        3.   Militarizing the Drug War
        4.   Deficiencies of High-Level Enforcement Strategies

    B.   Retail-Level Enforcement
        1.   Indiscreet Drug Dealing
        2.   Discreet Drug Dealing
        3.   Tactics
            a.   Street Sweeps
            b.   Buy and Bust
            c.   Reverse Stings
        4.   Benefits of Concentrated Enforcement
    C.   Efforts Aimed at Juveniles
        1.   Prevention
        2.   Maintaining Police Presence
        3.   Education
            a.   Drug Abuse Resistance Education (DARE)

III. Community Policing and the Drug Problem
    A.   Factors of Citizen Initiatives
    B.   What Community Policing Can Do
        1.   Addressing Discreet and Indiscreet Dealing
        2.   Gathering Information
        3.   Alternative Strategies
        4.   Police Presence
        5.   Community Participation
        6.   Harness the Vigilante Impulse
        7.   Control Corruption and Abuse of Authority
        8.   Reduce Profitability of Trafficking
        9.   Problem Solving
        10.   Focus on Youth Gangs
        11.   Focus on Juveniles
        12.   Work with Public and Private Agencies
        13.   Add Scope to Overall Police Effort
        14.   Reduce Risk of Civil Disturbances

IV. Summary

Review of Key Terms

Bureau of Alcohol, Tobacco, and Firearms
buy-bust
community policing
corruption
discreet
Drug Usage Forecast
Federal Bureau of Investigation
gangs
harm reduction
high-level enforcement
indiscreet
information

police presence
prevention
problem solving
racism
reverse stings
street sweeping
traditional policing
U.S. Customs Service
vigilante

1. In _____ operations, officers target an area and pose as buyers, after the transaction they arrest the seller.

2. Drug efforts targeting juveniles should focus on _____ as well as enforcement.

3. Drug dealing that occurs in homes, offices, bars and other locations is _____ dealing.

4. The _____ has the responsibility of interdicting drugs that are intermingled with exports coming into the country.

5. The switch from a traditional reactive approach to a _____ approach reorders priorities to place emphasis on helping people feel safer from the threats drugs pose.

6. The police should make _____ the criterion by which to guide drug enforcement planning, because police cannot completely eliminate drugs.

7. Community policing can make the best use of _____ to reduce open dealing.

8. The _____ works closely with state and local police agencies in attempting to target mid-level drug wholesalers and dealers.

9. Community policing can often gather better _____ than traditional undercover operations.

10. _____ is designed to attack the drug problem at the top of the drug trafficking hierarchy.

11. Kids join _____ for identity, for the recreational activities they provide, and for protection.

12. _____ drug dealing includes open street dealing, as well as crack houses and shooting galleries.

13. Police departments have traditionally been reluctant to involve officers in street-level anti-drug efforts for fear of _____.

14. Community policing can harness the _____ impulse and channel it in positive directions.

15. _____ is a method of targeting indiscreet dealing in the hope that this will at least drive it underground.

16. The _____ is responsible for attacking the criminal organizations that are responsible for distributing large quantities of drugs.

17. _____ can elicit information that _____ cannot because casual encounters on the streets are routine and drug dealers cannot identify police informants.

18. Fears, concerns, and reactions to drugs result in substantial levels of covert and overt _____.

19. _____ data shows that drugs play some immediate role in the lives of the vast majority of people arrested in major cities.

20. When officers pose as dealers and arrest the customer after the transaction it is a _____.

Review Questions

1. List the six goals that are useful in guiding police decisionmaking when implementing drug elimination strategies.

    (1) _____

    (2) _____

    (3) _____

    (4) _____

    (5) _____

    (6) _____

2. Describe why high-level enforcement strategies are within the purview of federal agencies.

    _____

    _____

    _____

    _____

3. List the federal enforcement agencies that are most responsible for high-level enforcement.

_____

_____

_____

_____

_____

_____

_____

4. List the three parts of the community policing approach that holds the most promise of making a long-term difference with the drug problem.

   (1) _____

   (2) _____

   (3) _____

5. Describe how community policing efforts can impact the profitability of drug dealing.

_____

_____

_____

_____

_____

_____

_____

_____

_____

_____

_____

_____

_____

_____

_____

_____

6. Describe how community policing's use of problem-solving techniques offers an effective means of responding to drug dealing.

_____

_____

_____

_____

_____

_____

_____

_____

_____

_____

_____

_____

_____

_____

_____

7. Describe how community policing can make the best use of police presence to reduce open drug dealing.

_____

_____

_____

_____

_____

_____

_____

_____

_____

_____

_____

_____

_____

_____

_____

Practical Exercises

1. Research the DARE program. Find the curriculum and examine the concepts and ideas DARE officers attempt to convey to children. Identify the reason this program has not been successful. What changes would you make to this educational approach that may be more effective?

2. Solve the following problem as an officer in a very small community in a rural area:

    The county in which you work as a CPO is widely known as a major marijuana producer. Several law enforcement officials have been convicted of various trafficking related charges stemming from federal law enforcement corruption probes. Local juries have never convicted a resident of marijuana related charges. This area is characterized by high poverty rates, high unemployment, lack of resources, and little industry. Local residents are not necessarily users of marijuana but they view growing it as their only income generating option. What can you do as a CPO to change public attitudes about marijuana growing? What underlying problems have to first be resolved to deal with this problem? Should the primary response be one of law enforcement?

3. As an officer in a medium-sized city, you have been assigned to deal with the following problem:

    Your department identified a "hot spot" of drug related activity in an area with several abandoned warehouses. The department implemented a plan for dealing with the situation that included a sweep and long term activities like increased patrol and working with a planning agency to find renters for the warehouses. This was achieved and that area has been successfully cleaned up. The problem you face is that the drug activity was simply displaced and is now located in an area on your beat.

    The new area is characterized by dilapidated homes that serve as drug houses. Much dealing is done in the open, including dealers selling their wares on street corners to passing motorists and pedestrians. Develop a long-term plan for cleaning up this area. How can you work with the community to aid in your efforts? What can you do to prevent simply displacing the problem? Use the three parts of the community-policing approach in your plan.

4. As a CPO in a small rural department, you have been assigned to deal with the following problem:

    Crystal Meth is a growing problem in your community. The local hospital has reported an increase in the number of emergency room patients who have overdosed. The high school has reported an increase in students who are experimenting with the drug. Your department has noticed a significant increase in the number of arrests for possession of the drug. Yet, there appears to be no pattern of use and sales based on geography. It is a county-wide problem.

You must develop a plan to determine the extent of the problem and then decide the best way to respond. Will you work with other agencies? How will you determine the primary users? What elements of the community policing approach will facilitate a successful response to this problem?

Chapter 10
Community Policing and Special Populations

Learning Objectives

After reading the chapter, you should be able to:

1. Describe community policing's ability to work with disenfranchised populations.

2. Identify and discuss the special nature of policing juveniles.

3. List the characteristics of a youth gang as well as the criteria for identifying gang members.

4. Understand why children join gangs.

5. Describe the tactics that have the potential to reduce gang problems.

6. Describe the difficulties inherent in policing the homeless.

7. Understand how community policy can respond to problems related to the homeless.

8. Describe the reasons for the hindered relationship between minorities and the police.

9. List the reasons race is a volatile police issue.

10. Describe the problems presented in policing undocumented immigrants.

11. Identify the responses police should incorporate when dealing with immigrant populations.

12. Identify the special problems presented by policing tourists and transients.

Chapter Outline

I. **Juveniles**
   A. Victimization
      1. Identifying Abused Children
      2. Parental Drug Problems
      3. Working with Social Service Agencies
      4. CPO as Community Liaison

II.   Juvenile Crime and Violence
  A.   Causal Factors
  B.   Working with Schools

III.   Urban Youth Gangs
  A.   Characteristics
  B.   Identifying Gang Members
  C.   Reasons Gangs Form
  D.   COP Intervention Programs
      1.   Tactics for Reducing Gang Problems

IV.   Policing the Homeless
  A.   Factors Leading to Increasing Population
  B.   Criminality
  C.   Victimization
  D.   CPO as Community Liaison
  E.   Typology of Homeless People

V.   Minorities and the Police
  A.   Reasons Race Is a Volatile Issue
  B.   Minority Complaints About the Police
  C.   Lightning Rods of Racial Tension
      1.   The Rodney King Incident
      2.   The Abner Louima Incident
      3.   The Amadou Diallo Incident
      4.   The Rampart Division Scandal
      5.   Driving While Black

VII.   Undocumented Immigrants
  A.   Victimization
  B.   Criminality
  C.   Police Priorities
  D.   Police Responses

VIII. Tourists and Transients
  A.   Reckless Behavior
  B.   Victimization
  C.   Protection

IX.   Summary

Review of Key Terms

child abuse
Community Action Team (CAT)
community liaison
disorganization
diversity

excessive force
homeless
Homeless Lifestyle
immigrants
juveniles
Office of Juvenile Justice and Delinquency Prevention
professional policing
Socioeconomic Homeless
tourists
undocumented immigrants
urban youth gangs

1. The _____ present a twofold problem for the police, due to the crimes they commit and the extraordinary levels of victimization.

2. _____ includes those who have chosen the streets as their lifestyle.

3. _____ have become one of law enforcement's most difficult problems and have spread to medium-sized cities.

4. _____ account for about two percent of the total U.S. population.

5. Gangs form because of _____ and disintegration that occur in neighborhoods.

6. In dealing with _____ the police are faced with a criminogenic population, but also a highly victimized population.

7. _____ are homeless as a result of losing a job, being under-employed, spouse abuse, or divorce.

8. Due to large numbers of _____, some resort cities have specialized problems.

9. One potential police response to aid in dealing with immigrant populations is to increase the _____ of the department's officers.

10. In the role of _____, a CPO can link families and juveniles in need with agencies that can help.

11. A _____ was established in Reno, Nevada to deal with the growing gang problem.

12. _____ plays a large role in delinquency and police should do more to identify and prosecute it.

13. The smuggling of _____ has become a major crime problem in the United States.

14. The traditional service orientation of the police disappeared when _____ came to dominate police thinking.

15. The _____ identified three components of an effective school-based gang control strategy.

16. One reason for minority complaints about police is the use of _____.

Review Questions

1. List the three general strategies police can use to protect children.

    (1) _____

    (2) _____

    (3) _____

2. List the four causal factors of juvenile violence according to the National Coalition of State Juvenile Justice Advisory Groups.

    (1) _____

    (2) _____

    (3) _____

    (4) _____

3. List the characteristics of street gangs.

    _____

    _____

    _____

    _____

    _____

4. List the five best criteria to be used by the police in identifying gang members.

    (1) _____

    (2) _____

    (3) _____

    (4) _____

    (5) _____

5. List the five tactics for reducing gang problems.

   (1) _____

   (2) _____

   (3) _____

   (4) _____

   (5) _____

6. Describe the six reasons for growing homeless populations nationwide.

   (1) _____

   (2) _____

   (3) _____

   (4) _____

   (5) _____

   (6) _____

7. List the reasons race is a volatile police issue.

_____

_____

_____

_____

_____

_____

_____

_____

8. What specific challenges do police face in dealing with undocumented immigrants?

_____

_____

_____

_____

_____

_____

_____

_____

9. What are the two problems police face in dealing with tourists and transients?

    (1) _____

    (2) _____

Practical Exercises

1. As an officer in a medium-sized city, your chief has given you the following assignment:

    You have been asked to develop a plan for preventing future criminality by providing services to victims of child abuse. Your department usually learns of victimized children from a social service agency. The primary police role at that point is to arrest the perpetrator(s) and assist the prosecution by investigating the abuse. Your chief would like to see a more proactive approach in identifying child victims and wants to work closely with other organizations to both identify the children and provide services.

    Identify the agencies the department should approach and develop a relationship with. What types of services should be offered to these children? Should the primary response to parents be one of law enforcement? Why? What services could the parents benefit from?

2. The medium-sized city in which you are a CPO has been faced with a recent increase in the number of Hispanic immigrants. Some of these people are in the country illegally, but the majority are here legally. Many of the immigrants are gainfully employed and most send a most of their income home to their families.

    There has been a series of armed robberies directed at the workers as they leave the banks and check cashing businesses in one geographic area. This did not come to police attention until a long pattern had been established because none of the robberies were reported. It wasn't until the county appointed a liaison to work with the immigrants that these robberies came to the attention of the department.

    Your fellow officers working the same beat have voiced concern over the large number of alcohol intoxication and public intoxication arrests they have made involving the immigrants. There has been very little violence among these people, however you are aware of the role alcohol plays in violent crime and want to address the issue before it becomes a problem.

    You are responsible for developing a response to these situations. You recognize that these new citizens are hesitant to contact the police out of fear and due to the language barrier. What underlying issues must the department respond to in addressing these situations? How can you develop a relationship with this community? What are your goals and how will you achieve them? Will you work with any other agencies in the community to offer services?

3. Business owners in the downtown area have made a series of complaints about the number of homeless people in the area. They claim that the recent increase in homeless in the area has lead to a decrease in the number of customers and subsequently, their profits. Some citizens have complained that they are afraid to shop in the area because of the homeless.

    Using the typology of homeless people from the text, determine the best possible response to this situation. You will need different plans for each type of person. You will need to work with private and public service agencies in determining a solution. What types of services would be most important overall and for the specific types? Do you utilize the law enforcement function at all? How do you best connect with the homeless community?

4. Your community of Playtona Beach, Florida receives a barrage of high school and college students each March and April. They come to have a good time and they go to great lengths to do it. They bring a lot of money to the area and they spend it freely. Hotel owners are satisfied with the current police response to the spring break crowds but other citizens are not. The population in Playtona is roughly 60 percent senior citizens and they are demanding that the police do more to control the behavior of these tourists. They have collectively complained that for two months in the spring they cannot access the beaches, many restaurants, and other businesses in the city. You realize that the tourists present a special situation, you must protect them, yet also monitor their behavior.

    How can the department best deal with this dilemma? How can the department facilitate a reconciliation between these two segments of Playtona? Is that necessary to solving this problem? Develop a problem-solving plan to resolve these issues.

5. After hearing about other departments' patterns of stopping drivers for "driving while black," your chief has decided that she wants you to find out if it is a problem in your city. You must develop a research plan to determine if the officers in your department are guilty of this making stops, writing citations, and making arrests based on race. How will you make this determination?

Chapter 11
Toward a New Breed of Police Officer

Learning Objectives

After reading the chapter, you should be able to:

1. Identify the two primary sources of individual images and impressions of police.

2. Describe why the police role is paradoxical.

3. Describe the role of patrol officers in traditional policing and implementing community policing.

4. Identify the characteristics of people who have traditionally entered policing.

5. Describe the nature of police work and the research techniques used to glean that information.

6. Discuss the impact of "danger" on the social isolation of police officers.

7. List and describe the reasons for resistance to community policing.

8. Describe the impact community policing has on the role of the police.

9. Identify the characteristics of the ideal candidate for a position in a community policing department.

Chapter Outline

I.   Images and Impressions
    A.   Herman Goldstein: Policing in a Free Society
    B.   Oversimplification of Police Roles

II.   Traditional Police Culture
    A.   Personalities of Individuals Seeking Policing Career
        1.   Idealism v. Authoritarianism
        2.   John Broderick
        3.   Carpenter and Raza

     B.   Mundane Nature of Daily Police Work
         1.   Studies of Activities
         2.   Poorly Structured Patrol Time
     C.   Police Officer Working Personality
         1.   "Danger"
         2.   Isolation
              a.   Symbols
              b.   Nature of Work
              c.   Paramilitary Bureaucracy

III.   Resistance to Community Policing
     A.   Internal Resistance
         1.   Traditional System
              a.   Reasons for Administrative Resistance
              b.   Reasons for Line Officer Resistance

IV.   Changing Traditional Police Culture
     A.   Broadening the Mandate
     B.   Officer Autonomy
     C.   Educated Officers

V.   What Community Policing Offers
     A.   Realistic Goals Aimed at Improving Quality of Life in Community
     B.   Shift From "Crime-Fighter" to Community Problem-Solver

VI.   Implications for the Future
     A.   Changes in Recruiting Efforts
         1.   Educated, Diverse Applicants
         2.   Independent Thinkers
         3.   Professionals
         4.   Continued Information Gathering Efforts of Officers
     B.   Difficulty of Keeping Officers
         1.   Insulating from Negative Police Culture
         2.   Other Employment Opportunities
         3.   Salary

Review of Key Terms

authoritarianism
autonomy
change
communication skills
cultural divide
cultural strings
danger
force
idealism
isolation

line officers
middle mangers
paradoxical
paramilitary bureaucracy
patrol officers
professional
protective cover
reactionary conservatives
reel life
rejection
social isolation
thin blue line
traditionalists

1. People who instinctively react in a conservative manner regardless of merit of their position and without reflecting upon consequences of their acts are sometimes referred to as _____.

2. The police are the only agents of formal social control with the right to use _____.

3. _____ reinforces the notion that people outside the police subculture are to be viewed warily as potential threats to officers physical or emotional well being.

4. Some resistance to community police stems from a general reluctance to embrace _____.

5. Our personalized picture of the police is the result of our real life experiences and _____ experiences which include the officers we have experienced in the theater and the media.

6. _____ stifles innovation and breeds immature personalities.

7. Some who resist community policing are referred to as _____ who feel that police departments should deal with "serious crime" and not broaden its mandate.

8. _____ are the backbone of the traditional police approach.

9. By emphasizing the crime-fighting role of the police, the public tends to view them as the _____ protecting good from evil.

10. Some argue that police impose social isolation upon themselves to protect against real and perceived dangers, and the loss of personal and professional _____.

11. Most resistance to community policing comes from _____.

12. Many who have entered police work exhibit a tendency toward conformity and _____, exhibiting conservative, aggressive, cynical and rigid behaviors.

13. _____ refers to the idea that when a problem develops a responsible party can deflect criticism by reassigning responsibility.

14. _____ is one of the most important facets in the development of a police working personality.

15. The _____ between line officers and administrators can widen if large numbers of line officers fail to embrace community policing.

16. The most critical determinant of a successful CPO is _____.

17. _____ by the community stems, in part, from the resentment that sometimes arises when laws are enforced.

18. Due to the freedom and autonomy given to line officers under community policing, the best candidates will be individuals who can function as true _____.

19. The threat of losing status and control, as well as sharing decision-making can lead to _____ failing to embracing community policing efforts.

20. The _____ that have traditionally held policing together (danger, isolation, control, authority) must be severed if community policing is to be successful.

21. The people who have traditionally entered police work share the qualities of _____ and authoritarianism.

22. The idea that the police represent a 'thin blue line' that protects civil liberties and is also the greatest threat to these liberties means the police may be seen as having _____ roles.

23. _____ is an emotional and physical condition that makes it difficult for members of one social group to have relationships and interact with members of another group.

Review Questions

1. What are the two types of individual experiences that culminate in our personal images and impressions of police?

    (1) _____

    (2) _____

2. Describe what is meant by the 'paradoxical roles' of the police.

_____

_____

_____

_____

_____

_____

_____

_____

3. Describe the characteristics of authoritarianism.

_____

_____

_____

_____

_____

_____

_____

_____

4. Describe the three ways Carpenter and Raza found that police applicants differ from other occupational groups.

(1) _____

(2) _____

(3) _____

5. List the six research techniques used to study police activity.

(1) _____

(2) _____

(3) _____

(4) _____

(5) _____

(6) _____

6. How does the police social role affect social isolation?

_____

_____

_____

_____

_____

_____

_____

_____

_____

_____

_____

_____

_____

_____

7. Describe the "new breed of police officer."

_____

_____

_____

_____

_____

_____

_____

_____

_____

_____

_____

_____

_____

_____

Practical Exercises

1. Interview two males and two females, if possible choose people of different races. Ask them to describe their images and impressions of police. Follow up with questions relating to their exposure to police officers throughout their lives. Determine if their impressions are most tied to their real-life or reel-life experiences.

2. The new chief in your medium-sized department has publicly announced the implementation of community policing and has appointed you to the committee that will oversee this effort. Your survey of line and supervisory officers indicates that there is much support among middle managers, but the line officers are very skeptical of these efforts. Detail a plan to educate these officers about community policing. Identify what can be done to reassure line officers and win their support. Be sure to identify the potential problems associated with the lack of line officer support for the initiatives and address each in your plan.

3. As the new recruiting officer in a medium-sized department, you are faced with the task of recruiting applicants to fill 20 new positions. The applicant files you have reviewed in the initial stages are predominately those of white males with high school diplomas and no policing experience.

   Using the information in the text, identify the optimal characteristics of the applicants you seek. Devise a strategy to reach this type of applicant. Where can you find these people and how can you convince them to apply for the job? Keep in mind that retention is sometimes as difficult as recruiting. Include in your recruiting plan the issues that must be addressed to assure that your department retains these officers once they are hired.

4. As the recruiting officer for your department, you hope to convince your chief that hiring college educated officers in the best interest of the department and the community. Using information from the text, write an essay that describes the benefits of this new breed of police officer.

Chapter 12
Community Policing at the Crossroads

Learning Objectives

After reading the chapter, you should be able to:

1. Describe the academic criticisms directed at community policing.

2. Understand the paradigmatic shift resulting from community policing.

3. List and describe the seven value changes necessary for community policing.

4. List the six structural issues associated with community policing.

5. Describe the social issues that lead to community policing.

6. Understand the role of the Community Resource Centers in the early idea of community policing.

7. Describe early attempts designed to resolve problems between the police and community and the shadow they cast on community policing.

8. Describe the contemporary issues and questions about community policing.

9. Discuss what community policing offers in terms of "community security" in light of terrorism.

Chapter Outline

I. **Community Policing: From Theory to Practice**
    A.   Scholarly Response

II. **A Restatement of the Philosophy of Community Policing**
    A.   Paradigm Shift
    B.   Human and Social Problems Focus
    C.   Service and Problem Solving
    D.   Changes in Values
    E.   Structural Issues

III. **The Social Context of the Community Policing Revolution**
    A.   Police as Crime-fighters
    B.   Volatile Police-Community Relations
    C.   Outside Pressure
    D.   Private Security

IV. **Turning the Spirit of Community Policing into Practice**
    A.   Proactive Outreach Efforts
        1.   Community Resource Centers
        2.   Social Agents
        3.   Racism

V. **Challenges to the Spirit of Community Policing**
    A.   Police Community Relations
    B.   Team Policing

VI. **Contemporary Issues and Questions About Community Policing**
    A.   Service Ethos
    B.   Responsibility of Service Agencies
    C.   Human Activities
    D.   Science and Bureaucracy
    E.   Leaders of the Community
    F.   Accountability
    G.   Trends that Undermine the Spirit of Community Policing
        1.   Metaphors
        2.   Quality of Life
        3.   Safety Seekers
        4.   Social Ordering
        5.   Democracy
        6.   Community Needs and Desires
        7.   Equal Partnerships and Social Control

VII. **Community policing and Terrorism**
A. What Community Policing Offers

VIII. **Summary**

Review of Key Terms

accountability
community policing
community relations
Community Resource Centers
decentralization
ethos of service
first responders
paradigm
patrol

people
private security
police orientation
Problem Analysis Advisory Committee (PAAC)
resources
rule of law
safety seekers
social agents
Support Services Committee
team policing

1. Community policing redefines power, control, and _____.

2. Removing _____ from the community also removed a visible symbol of social control.

3. _____ was an important attempt to change the focus and structure of the police but failed to capture the imagination or organization of the police.

4. We are becoming a society of _____ and risk managers because of the unrealistic fear of crime.

5. The idea of _____ is a radical departure from traditional notions of policing.

6. The growth of _____ was a growing threat to the police, as wealthy citizens were turning away from public protection.

7. Early efforts at improving _____ were viewed as "eyewash and whitewash."

8. Norfolk implemented a _____, a citywide body that provides services and resolves neighborhood problems.

9. Community policing seeks to inject an _____ into a culture that has historically focused on crime.

10. _____ were important to the early philosophy of community police and were viewed as proactive outreach efforts.

11. Community policing calls for the _____ of police organizations in a manner that police officers on the street have greater organizational power.

12. Community policing involves a dramatic shifting of _____ and public preoccupation with crime control to a broader range of activities.

13. The San Diego Police Department implemented a _____ where participants problem-solve disorder problems.

14. Community policing is a _____ shift that challenges long-standing conceptualizations of the police and fundamental assumptions about doing police work.

15. Community policing requires changes in the way that police _____ are spent.

16. _____, not the police, have the ultimate power to control crime.

17. Community policing involves a detachment of the police institution from the strict _____ and its professional crime fighting orientation.

18. Community policing requires a reordering of _____ deployment, to free line officers to serve as outreach specialists.

19. Community policing can aid in community security because line officers can be better _____ when they are given decision-making authority.

Review Questions

1. What are the two groups that find their power and control reduced as a result of community policing?

    (1) _____

    (2) _____

2. List the seven basic values of community policing.

    (1) _____

    (2) _____

    (3) _____

    (4) _____

    (5) _____

    (6) _____

    (7) _____

3. List the six structural issues associated with community policing.

    (1) _____

    (2) _____

    (3) _____

    (4) _____

    (5) _____

    (6) _____

4. List the six contemporary issues related to community policing.

    (1) _____

    (2) _____

    (3) _____

    (4) _____

    (5) _____

    (6) _____

5. List the seven trends that undermine the spirit of community policing.

    (1) _____

    (2) _____

    (3) _____

    (4) _____

    (5) _____

    (6) _____

    (7) _____

6. List the six ways community policing can improve community security.

    (1) _____

    (2) _____

    (3) _____

    (4) _____

    (5) _____

    (6) _____

Practical Exercises

1. Find two early and contemporary articles from academic journals about community policing. Compare the concepts and strategies in each. Do you recognize any key differences? Similarities? Which are most practical? Which would be easiest to implement?

2. As a CPO in a large department, you are stationed at a satellite station located in your racially mixed beat. This freestanding structure serves as a community resource center and a very small police station. It has been in existence for two years and the department is calling it a success. You, however, have noticed that it is the same small group of white business owners and home owners who attend meetings and organize activities.

    Is this a successful effort? Are the true sentiments of the community being voiced and responded to? What can be done to include other groups in the neighborhood? How can you encourage their involvement?

3. Your chief has assigned you to design a Community Resource Center for your beat that is characterized by high poverty and unemployment rates. It is a predominately African-American community and most citizens have little access to health care, job training, education, and transportation. What services do you feel would be important? Which outside agencies would you involve in the center? What would be the first priority? What steps would you take to get input from the community? What role would the community play in the design and implementation? How would you measure success?

4. You have been asked to develop a plan for increasing your department's interaction with the community regarding terrorism. Using the information from the text, and the philosophies of community policing, how can you work with the community to encourage citizens' feelings of security while alleviating fear of terrorism? How can you involve the community without fostering fears?

Answer Key

CHAPTER 1

Review of Key Terms

1. Community policing
2. programmatic facet
3. aggressive tactics
4. proactive
5. professional model
6. order maintenance
7. community engagement
8. Broken Windows
9. decentralize
10. strategic facet
11. problem-oriented policing
12. philosophy
13. philosophical facet
14. zero tolerance
15. law enforcement function
16. organizational and personnel facet
17. fear of crime
18. situational crime prevention

Review Questions

1. It broadens the police mission from a narrow focus on crime to a mandate that encourages the police to explore creative solutions for community concerns.

2. The introduction has been a long, complicated process. Some departments have used community policing as a cover for aggressive law enforcement tactics. Many police agencies have adopted the language of community policing but have not changed organizational structures. Community policing threatens the status quo. Community policing may generate public expectations that go unfulfilled.

3. broad police function and community focus; citizen input; working together; developing trust; sharing power; creativity; neighborhood variation

4. geographic focus and ownership; direct, daily, face-to-face contact; prevention focus

5. reoriented police operations; problem-solving and situational crime prevention; community engagement

6. a technique; public relations; soft on crime; flamboyant; paternalistic; independent within the department; cosmetic; social work; elitist; a panacea; safe; a series or bundle of programs; problem-oriented policing

7. Weed and seed is a two-pronged approach to crime control. Law enforcement attempts to "weed out" criminals from an area. "Seeding brings prevention, intervention, treatment, and neighborhood revitalization to the area.

CHAPTER 2

Review of Key Terms

1. Spoils Era
2. Sir Robert Peel
3. self-preservation
4. Industrial Revolution
5. August Vollmer
6. Civil Rights Act of 1871
7. justice of the peace
8. Metropolitan Police Act of 1829
9. New Left
10. Police Community Relations (PCR)
11. Volstead Act of 1919
12. team policing
13. Crime Prevention Units
14. Civil Service
15. isolation
16. vigilantism
17. Kerner Commission
18. Law Enforcement Assistance Act (LEAA)
19. blue laws

Review Questions

1. continued population growth; the shift from an agrarian to an industrial economy; increased complexity in the distribution of material resources; the crowding of people into cities; and advances in technology

2. citizens were responsible for law and order among themselves; the system of the justice of the peace; a paid police force

3. It was a period prior to the Civil Service Act of 1883 when politicians solidified power by taking care of those who helped them win elections.

4. *Self-preservation:* citizens must be willing to kill or be killed, when the official system fails to provide adequate protection; *Right of revolution:* when something fails to work properly, revolution is as valid a response as reform; *Economic rationale:* maintaining an effective criminal justice system is an expensive proposition

5. remove politics from police organizations; select a chief based on competence; physical and character qualifications for patrol officers; salaries that permit a decent living standard; adequate training for recruits and officers; a communication system; complete records; a crime-prevention unit; state police forces for rural areas; state bureaus of criminal investigation in every state

6. authorization; function; organizational design; demand for services; relationship to environment; tactics/technology; outcomes

7. improve communication, reduce hostility, and identify tensions between police and community; assist the police and community in acquiring skills to remove crime detection and prevention; define the police role, emphasizing equal protection; adopt a teamwork approach; each officer should have a proper attitude and appreciation of community relations; enhance mutual understanding between the police and community; stress that administration of justice is a total community responsibility

8. race riots; Civil Rights Movement; Vietnam War and draft protests

9. isolation of the police from the public; a growing use of overt and symbolic violence to control groups in society

CHAPTER 3

Review of Key Terms

1. adversarial
2. blockbusting
3. inclusion
4. threat of crime
5. hierarchy
6. underclass
7. Chicago School
8. initiatives
9. social interactions
10. community relationships

11. legal constructs
12. natural community
13. neighborhood
14. Kurt Vonnegut

Review Questions

1. any area in which people with a common culture share common interests

2. a particular geographic area where a group of people lives; a legal entity or unit of governance; social interactions that include a division of labor and sense of interdependence; individuals who have a shared culture, interest, outlook or perspective; a place where values are transmitted; social interactions collectively shape its character; the processes of inclusion and exclusion; shared sentiment, a sense of belonging

3. presence or absence of businesses; location of churches, schools, community associations; residential groupings and points of transition; homogeneity of economic, occupational, or ethnic characteristics; physical characteristics; and a collection of shared interests

4. affordable technology, such as the automobile, the telephone, and the Internet allow those with sufficient resources to make bonds based on community of interest without regard for geography or dependency

5. *Underclass:* inner-city neighborhoods; loss of anchors, fear of interaction and rebuilding sense of community; *Middle class:* wide range of options, suburban enclaves, resources for interaction; *Upper class:* can afford security, have means to travel to community of interest, affect social policy

6. to revive the idea that those who live in the same area can improve the quality of life by understanding how they share a community of mutual interest

7. with face-to-face contacts and meetings with average citizens

CHAPTER 4

Review of Key Terms

1. non-controntive communication skills.
2. socioeconomic status
3. the Mollen Commission
4. Authoritarianism
5. Rampart scandal
6. symbolic assailants
7. excessive force
8. police corruption

Review Questions

1. It affects public participation in crime reduction programs, political support for the police, police programs, and crime-related legislation. It is also a key consideration when making budgetary and operational decisions.

2. greater cooperation; decrease in crime rate; more effective enforcement; better communication; improved working relationships between citizens and official groups; more people interested in police careers; increased governmental support for new police programs

3. Older people tend to view police more positively than younger people. Younger people are more involved in dangerous behavior and have more negative contacts with police. They are more likely to be victimized and are distrustful of authority figures.

4. Minorities view police positively, but less positively than whites. Race is the best predictor of citizen attitudes toward police. This is due to the perception that minorities are mistreated more frequently by police.

5. There is no difference by gender, they tend to view police the same. Citizens from lower socioeconomic backgrounds are less likely to view the police positively.

6. excessive force; police corruption; rudeness; authoritarianism; politics

CHAPTER 5

Review of Key Terms

1. leadership
2. role
3. structure
4. comprehensive model
5. neighborhood counsels
6. COMPSTAT
7. division of labor
8. active supervisors
9. classical organizational theory
10. evaluating
11. territorial imperative
12. organic organizations
13. commander profile report
14. quality circles
15. authority
16. community partnership; problem solving
17. bean counting

Review Questions

1. the organization follows the principle of hierarchy; specialization or division of labor exists whereby individuals are assigned a limited number of job tasks and responsibilities; official policies and procedures guide the activities of the organization; administrative acts, decisions, and rules are recorded in writing; authority within the organization is associated with one's position; candidates are appointed on the basis of their qualifications, and training is a necessary part of the selection process

2. arrest; citation; advise to file restraining order; prove service; provide information

3. traditional; innovative; supportive; active

4. performance gap; recognizing a need for change; creating a proper climate for change; diagnosing the problem; identifying alternative strategies; selecting the strategy; determining and operationalizing implementation strategy; evaluating and modifying the strategy

CHAPTER 6

Review of Key Terms

1. societal problems
2. geographic concentration pattern
3. hot spot
4. response
5. community partnerships
6. citizen surveys
7. community meetings
8. prevention efforts
9. Newport News, Virginia
10. crime analysis
11. problem solving
12. problems
13. dangerous place
14. New York City Police Department
15. reactive
16. scanning
17. third party policing

Review Questions

1. Rather than simply reacting to calls for service, the police actively work to prevent crime and improve neighborhood conditions that are conducive to crime. Prevention efforts must focus on specific problems as opposed to distributing efforts randomly.

    The police must recognize that there are many conditions within society that contribute to crime and disorder. The police must analyze these conditions and develop specific responses to each problem or situation rather than depending on rapid response and answering calls for service.

    Crime and disorder problems, are the result of innumerous societal problems at are outside the control of the police. The police must engage and cooperate with other social agencies to develop a unified strategy for attacking complex problems.

2. *Scanning:* the process whereby individual officers, police units, or the police department collectively examines the jurisdiction for problems or hot spots; *Analysis:* learning the who, what, when, where, and how about the problem; *Response:* developing an effective means of dealing with the problem, preferably with citizen help; *Assessment:* determining if the response worked to eliminate or reduce the problem.

3. officer observation and experience; citizen complaints and community groups; crime mapping; police reports, calls for service analysis, and crime analysis; citizen surveys

4. by time period; by shift or watch; by beat or district; around a hot spot concentrations in an area over time; compare police activities with social and ecological characteristics

5. geographic concentration patterns and similar offense patterns

6. Officers Lack the Analytical Skills Needed; Managers and Supervisors Do Not Know How; Agencies Resist Change; Heavy Workloads; Little Community Involvement; Little Support for Governmental Agencies; Circumstantial Problems; Linear Process; Too Little is Known About the Problem

CHAPTER 7

Review of Key Terms

1. motor patrol
2. rapid response
3. crime-fighters
4. Uniform Crime Reports; Index
5. mandate; mission
6. deterrence

7. outreach specialists
8. status offenses
9. Kansas City Preventive Patrol study
10. professional policing model
11. juveniles
12. opportunity-reduction
13. RAND
14. Minneapolis Experiment
15. context

Review Questions

1. reported crime rates; overall arrests; clearance rates; response times

2. murder; rape; robbery; aggravated assault; burglary; larceny; motor vehicle theft; arson

3. prevention of crime; intervention during the commission of a crime; resolution of the situation after the fact

4. rates of crimes reported showed no difference among the beats; victimization studies showed the proactive approach made no discernible impact on the kinds of crimes considered to be most susceptible to deterrence through preventive motor patrol; citizen attitudes toward police showed few consistent differences and no apparent pattern across the three different types of beats; fear of crime did not decline; citizen satisfaction with police did not improve in the experimental areas; and experimental conditions showed no effect on police response times or citizen satisfaction with response times

5. apathy; skepticism about police ability to do anything; notification of other people before calling police

6. unsolvable; solvable; already solved

7. It can help address some of the underlying problems in a community.

CHAPTER 8

Review of Key Terms

1. moral panics
2. victimization
3. Newark Fear Reduction Campaign
4. routine preventive patrol
5. Figgie Report
6. media
7. under-enforcement

8. fear of crime
9. Citizen Oriented Police Enforcement (COPE)
10. formless fear
11. law enforcement community
12. primary victimization
13. community policing
14. Flint Foot Patrol Experiment
15. Community Organizing Response Team (CORT)
16. secondary victimization
17. age
18. concrete fear
19. gender
20. wealth
21. property; violent

Review Questions

1. the Depression and Prohibition

2. victim precipitation

3. people in large cities; the young; women; those with more formal education; African-Americans

4. those with the lowest incomes; blue-collar workers; those with the least education; those who do not work full time; those who experienced a marital loss; the elderly

5. ordering fear of crime by age and gender are the exact opposite of victimization rates; fear of crime is higher than the victimization rate; fear patterns within the general population do not match victimization patterns

6. fear destroys the sense of community; prosperous citizens take more protective actions to safeguard themselves; fear hardens attitudes toward criminal, the poor and those who are different; fear can undermine citizen faith in the police and courts; fear has detrimental psychological effects on people; fear victims alter their habits and lifestyles

7. locale; degree of randomness; the bizarreness or violence associated with the act

8. The Victimization Model; The Disorder Model; The Community Concern Model; The Subcultural-Diversity Model

CHAPTER 9

Review of Key Terms

1. buy-bust
2. prevention
3. discreet
4. U.S. Customs Service
5. problem solving
6. harm reduction
7. police presence
8. Bureau of Alcohol, Tobacco, and Firearms
9. information
10. high-level enforcement
11. gangs
12. indiscreet
13. corruption
14. vigilante
15. street sweeping
16. Federal Bureau of Investigation
17.
18. racism
19. Drug Usage Forecast
20. reverse stings

Review Questions

1. reduce gang violence associated with trafficking and prevent emergence of organized crime groups; control street crimes committed by users; improve health, economic, and social well-being of users; restore the quality of life in communities; prevent children from experimenting with drugs; protect the integrity of criminal justice institutions

2. These investigations are time-consuming and expensive. Federal agencies have more resources.

3. Drug Enforcement Agency; Federal Bureau of Investigation; Bureau of Alcohol, Tobacco, and Firearms; U.S. Customs Service

4. law enforcement; drug education; drug treatment

5. Street-level enforcement strategies and police presence can reduce demand, thereby decreasing profit.

6. Departments using problem solving can alter strategies and implement programs based on the needs and desires of the community; they do not have to rely on traditional reactive approaches.

7. By working with a neighborhood group, they can make sweeps, and make dealers nervous. The goal is to give the appearance of having dealers under surveillance.

CHAPTER 10

Review of Key Terms

1. homeless
2. Homeless Lifestyle
3. urban youth gangs
4. undocumented immigrants
5. disorganization
6. juveniles
7. Socioeconomic Homeless
8. tourists.
9. diversity
10. community liaison
11. Community Action Team (CAT)
12. child abuse
13. immigrants
14. professional policing
15. Office of Juvenile Justice and Delinquency Prevention
16. excessive force

Review Questions

1. be more active in identifying abused children; cooperate with social agencies.; link families to agencies who can help

2. abuse and neglect; economic, social, educational conditions; gangs; accessibility of weapons

3. recognizable symbols; geographic territory; regular meeting pattern; organized, continuous course of criminality

4. admits being a gang member; has tattoos associated with a gang; police records or observations confirm association; has been arrested with gang members; a reliable informant confirms gang membership

5. target, arrest, incarcerate gang leaders; refer fringe members and their parents to services; provide preventative services; crisis intervention or mediation of gang fights; patrols of community

6. shortage of affordable housing; depopulation of mental hospitals; cuts to budgets of federal programs; unemployed or underemployed; low minimum wage; breakdown of traditional family

7. alarming rates of victimization of minorities; disproportionate number of minorities arrested and incarcerated; debate about promoting and hiring minorities; concern over racially motivated incidents; new militant groups that advocate violence against minorities

8. The fear of deportation makes them vulnerable to victimization.

9. criminality and victimization

CHAPTER 11

Review of Key Terms

1. reactionary conservatives
2. force
3. social isolation
4. change
5. reel life
6. paramilitary bureaucracy
7. traditionalists
8. patrol officers
9. thin blue line
10. autonomy
11. line officers
12. authoritarianism
13. protective cover
14. danger
15. cultural divide
16. communication skills
17. rejection
18. professionals
19. middle managers
20. cultural strings
21. idealism
22. paradoxical
23. isolation

Review Questions

1. real life and reel life

2. Police represent the 'thin blue line' that protects civil liberties, yet they are the greater threat to these liberties.

3. conservative, aggressive, cynical, rigid behaviors

4. police applicants are psychologically healthy; police applicants are more homogeneous; police are more like military personnel in their conformance to authority

5. radio calls from dispatchers to patrol cars; telephone calls by citizens to the police; dispatch records; observational data; self-reports from police officers; telephone interviews of citizens

6. They have a legal monopoly on the sanctioned use of violence.

7. educated; professional; diverse ethnic and racial background; excellent communication skills

CHAPTER 12

Review of Key Terms

1. accountability
2. social agents
3. team policing
4. safety seekers
5. community policing
6. private security
7. community relations
8. Support Services Committee
9. ethos of service
10. Community Resource Centers
11. decentralization
12. police orientation
13. Problem Analysis Advisory Committee (PAAC)
14. paradigm
15. resources
16. people
17. rule of law
18. patrol
19. first responders

Review Questions

1. local political officials; the rich and powerful

2. people deserve a say in how they are policed; people have the power to control crime; people are the reason for policing; people supervise and assess police performance; officers must be educated as community leaders; police executives must demonstrate commitment to the philosophy; police executives must shift to emphasize trust while maintaining accountability

3. changes in the way resources are spent; reordering of police work to allow time for problem solving; decentralization of organization power for purpose of addressing social problems; flattening the organizational structure of police departments; educating the public on the nature of police work as it relates to changes in response to calls for service; new system of accountability to allow citizens direct input in evaluating police

4. detachment from the strict rule of law and crime fighting to develop a service ethos; shifting responsibility for crime control to citizens and service agencies; shifting of police orientation with crime control to broad range of human activities; embracing science and bureaucratic efficiency; the adoption of imagery of service provisions and problem solving; the language of community-based accountability

5. The use of dangerous metaphors; police have failed to define "quality of life"; we are a society of safety seekers; we are destroying community as we reorder policing and society; policing is not democratic; not reading community needs and desires; not all partnerships are created equal

6. decentralization allows for faster response to crisis; officers are dispersed across community; line officers can be trained as first responders; use of fixed geographic beats allows officers to identify risks; CPOs are more trusted by citizens' CPOs can pursue leads